SHOW YOUR ASK!

Using Your Voice to Advocate for Yourself and Your Career

Joyel Crawford

ISBN: 9798491935468

This book is dedicated to God who made me, my parents who raised me and my husband, Jake who unconditionally loves me.

Show Your Ask!

Using Your Voice to Advocate for Yourself and Your Career

Introduction

My father always used to say, "You get what you ask for." I didn't understand it at the time. He shared a lot of sage wisdom that was like a boomerang that would come back and hit me over the head years later. This piece of advice must have been embedded in my subconscious like a sleeping giant because whenever I was challenged in life or my career- I found that merely asking a question would give me what I was seeking at that moment. It may have been clarity, consideration for a raise, more support, or less support (depending on who I was reporting to at the time). Asking for what I wanted also amplified my voice, empowered me, empowered others, and provided life-changing results that I don't think I would have encountered if I had not just asked.

My mission on this earth is to motivate and inspire others to manage their lives to the best of their abilities and become great leaders in the world.

My mission statement didn't come to me overnight. The idea came when I was in my most vulnerable state, trying to figure things out. I was at the lowest point in my life. I was experiencing work burnout and realized that my job and my choices were literally killing me. I remember shouting up to the heavens, in a wailing cry, asking God why I was put here to be in so much pain. The question reverberated off the walls. The pain echoed in my ears as if to answer; no one should ever feel the way I did at that moment. I didn't know it at the time, but I had lost myself. I had lost my voice. The engine that had pushed me along for so many years had stopped, and I didn't know how I was going to get it back on track. But I knew at that moment that I wasn't going to allow others to experience this pain.

When I was progressing in my career, there were no books about the importance of your voice and how it is a catalyst in your career and personal life. My intention with this book is to help you understand how important your voice can be. Even if you lose your voice, you can always find it.

Chapter One: Show Your Ask

From the first day of my first job out of college, I knew what I wanted to do next. Not many people get this lucky. But on my first day of work at my Big Girl Job, there was a person at the front of the room who spoke with passion and enthusiasm to educate and motivate us. And I knew that was what I wanted to do next.

I remember telling my new manager on Day One that I wanted to do what that guy in the front of the room was doing. My manager told me that I would need to pursue a career in Human Resources, which is "virtually impossible," or the Training Department, which was also hard to break into. But she stressed that I needed to focus on the job I was hired to do first, which was to be a Customer Service Representative for a Telecommunications Company. I told her not to get used to me being there because I was going to be a Trainer in the Human Resources Department.

I'm sure she was thinking, "Wow, she's got a lot of nerve coming in here telling me what she's going to do." But I didn't waiver. I knew I needed to bring my best to my new job every day until I became a Human Resources Trainer- even if it was "virtually impossible" to break into that department. *You've got to try to fail.* Making the first step is great but taking the second step is just as important. *Action builds momentum, which inspires more action.* I had no problem telling each of my supervisors what my path was going to be. But I also assured them that I was going to do my best while I was there so I wouldn't let the team down.

But how do you do it? How do you Show Your Ask?

Prepare, Present, Observe, and Close

Prepare

Think about you. Put yourself first for a moment. What does success look like to you? When I was envisioning my next role or project. I did some daydreaming and brainstorming. Put your good old pen to paper. What do you really need? Think about the basics. Is it more time, more money, more support, or more autonomy? When you really sit down and think about that, envision the outcomes of this discussion. Will you be more productive? Will the company be more productive?

Think about your special sauce or shine. What is the value that you bring to the table? Make a DIG (Damn, I'm Good) Folder. One of my Fairygodmentors, Wendy Wollner coined this term. On my career journey, I had a JIG (Joy is Great) Folder but DIG just sounds better, doesn't it? And it's reflective of what's inside. It's a place where you track your results, daily or on a regular basis; based on accomplishments, you collect testimonials from happy clients or customers, performance ratings, etc. Having your information handy is not only going to keep you prepared for career development discussions, salary negotiations, and interviews, but it is also a great confidence booster. When you gloss over all you have done, you will be saying it aloud. Declare it! "Damn, I'm Good!"

When you're thinking about preparation, also think about the other party. This could be your manager, a future employer, a client, or a co-worker. What does success look like for them? What do they really need from you? It's also a good time to think about how you got to discussing your ask. What is the background story of this discussion? Did a particular incident occur to trigger the conversation? It is helpful to recall this information because it may help you with your opening.

Present

As a professional actor... wait! You don't know that I love to act and have even gotten paid for it from time to time! I'm sure you've seen me. You may have to pause the video to catch me!

Anyway, as I was saying, as a professional actor, you have to prepare your script, song, etc., to win the director and production staff over. It is best not to audition cold. Just like a well-prepared actor, you can't walk into a negotiation conversation, interview, or career development unprepared. You need a script to refer to during meetings. This will help you to speak with confidence and avoid power-robbing words like 'I can't,' 'I wish,' 'I hope,' 'I'll try,' 'I should, or I would.' Speak with confidence and let the script be your anchor to keep you on track, especially if emotions begin to run high. Finally, you want to ensure you are speaking to the other person's interests. Tune into ME-FM. The call letters are WIIFM. (What's In It For Me) What's the value of this ASK to the other party?

I remember complaining to the Executive Director of Human Resources, one of my sponsors, about how much I was doing while not getting recognized for promotions. She said to me, "Joyel, this is all well and good. You've shared what you've done for you and your career, but what have you done for the business?" To her, I must have sounded like an opera singer singing "Me Me Me!" the whole time. Her question provided a lot of clarity. How was I positioning myself for these ASKS? What was the value proposition for the other party who was making the decisions? From then on, as I prepared, I made it a point to focus on the opportunity. How will this benefit the organization, team, or manager?

Oh, and I don't want to forget this nugget of advice: When presenting to leadership, **give them the greatest hits**, short bits of specific information. I mastered this by actively listening to how leaders communicate with others, their teams, and in meetings. Share the information the way they need to hear it. Short and sweet.

Observe

When emotions are running high (and even when they're not), make sure to check yourself before you wreck yourself. Self-awareness and self-management are two elements of emotional intelligence that are key to managing your emotions. What emotions are showing up for this meeting? How are you managing the emotions that are bubbling up for you?

Now that you're in this conversation, you know you will need to take a step back, listen closely, and take notes. Take a pause for the cause and take in their response. If warranted, respond with enthusiasm, then clarify any project details, offer, or action plan. If needed, ask for additional time to continue the discussion. Sidenote: I highly suggest that you don't accept a job offer on the spot! You may not have heard all of the pertinent details of the offer. It's best to get the offer in writing and give yourself time to digest all that was discussed.

What if you get a NO to your ASK? A very wise man gave this wonderful advice. ***NO equals Next Opportunity.*** It could be a good idea, but it may be bad timing. If you got a 'no' be professionally persistent. Follow up on it. But also think about whether or not this is the hill you want to die on. If this is a 'no,' for a salary increase or some special project, make sure you shared the value you bring to the team/company/manager. Go back to the videotape. Refer to your DIG Folder and highlight your experiences so that you can revisit why the ASK is good for both of you.

Close

You're almost in the home stretch! You need to lock this conversation, agreement, negotiation, or professional development plan down. Review what was discussed. Clarify any ambiguity. Document the key points discussed and agreed upon and, if appropriate, send the discussion summary to the other party. This is a great technique to also use if you are a people leader and have corrective action or performance improvement plan discussions.

TAKE FIVE!

1. Did you prepare supporting data for your ASK? What are the greatest hits?

_____

_____

_____

_____

_____

_____

_____

2.   What are you presenting to your
      manager/organization/team? What is the value
      proposition? Did you create a script?

_____

_____

_____

_____

_____

_____

_____

3.   What do you plan to observe during this
     conversation?

_____

_____

_____

_____

_____

_____

_____

4.   How will you close the conversation? Is everyone clear about the expectations?

_____

_____

_____

_____

_____

_____

5. Did you remember to keep a positive attitude and strategy by focusing on how both parties can win? What is the win-win strategy?

_____

_____

_____

_____

_____

_____

Chapter Two: Finding Your Voice

In addition to acting, I love to sing and publicly speak. I was born three months premature at two pounds and ten ounces. The doctors said I had powerful lungs. I came into this world belting out a tune of strength. I had something to say on Day One of my life and still think about the message I was sent here to share.

People loved to hear me speak and sing at festivals and competitions. I love using my voice every chance I have. But there were times when I wasn't as confident in sharing my voice.

I grew up in a two-parent home. My father is from Jamaica, and I am a first-generation American on his side of the family. Education is a part of our family's brand. It was never a question of IF I was going to college. It was a matter of WHEN. I was raised Roman Catholic and went to Catholic schools from kindergarten to high school. I was always one of a very few Black children in the class. Being the "only one" was something that came with the territory. My sister and I were raised to speak the King's English. It was how we spoke. Poor grammar usage was always corrected, and it never dawned on me that speaking this way would be the cause of ridicule and teasing.

I recall my fifth-grade teacher shouting at me one day in front of the class that if I said 'ax' one more time, she would 'get an ax and cut off my head.' Although my mother said the incident was unprofessional and borderline racially-biased, my fifth-grade mind interpreted it as her wanting me to improve my speech so people could understand me clearly.

As I kept using my voice, some didn't appreciate the King's English. I was teased for speaking 'too White,' and I started to retreat from being outspoken to muting myself. My reasoning was the less that I talked, the less I was teased. It was a complete contradiction from my extroverted self.

I would often count to five before asking questions. I don't know why the number five. Maybe it was just enough time to breathe and find the confidence to ask what I wanted to ask. My parents noticed me retreating and shying away from speaking up, so; they thrust me into speaking opportunities to grow my confidence. Suddenly, I was in original oratory and singing competitions and the lector at church. I would practice reading the Biblical text during the weekend or coming of age books aloud to my mom while she cooked dinner. She would correct me or educate me on words that were hard to pronounce or understand.

I didn't know it at the time, but my parents were building my confidence to use my voice again. As I grew stronger and more confident, I started to ask for and crave opportunities to use my voice. Winning those competitions made the peer jeers less audible, and soon after, others were asking me to help them present and speak publicly. When people would ask in amazement how I began speaking so well, I would always respond, "practice." I am thankful that my parents gave me the space and grace to practice.

There was a very sad day when I almost lost my voice forever. I was about 13 years into my career, and I was pretty miserable. My voice was more hoarse than usual, and it was hard for me to develop sound when I spoke or sang. I went to an Ear, Nose, and Throat Specialist who did a scope of my vocal cords and found a small pre nondual edema. I was forming a node. This can be the kiss of death for a singer and speaker. I remember when Julie Andrews' voice never recovered from her nodule surgery. Of course, my mind jumped straight to surgery! I asked the doctor if the condition could be reversed. She advised vocal rest for two weeks straight, which meant I couldn't work because my work consisted of talking and counseling others. No singing meant no life!

I'll never forget that day. I went back to my car in the pouring rain, thinking the weather was representative of my emotions pouring out of my body. The first person I called after getting the news was my manager at work. I was sobbing into the phone. I was going to need medical accommodations not to speak most of the day. I texted my friends about this horrific situation, and they met me with empathy, pads of paper, and markers so that I could communicate through writing. I asked my friends for support, and to keep me social because I knew staying at home speechless would push me further down the rabbit hole of despair.

My voice was everything. I had finally come to love it. For me, not having the ability to use my voice was the end of the world. At least it felt that way. My voice helped me be visible, heard, and respected, but now it was gone. Or it had the possibility of being gone forever if I didn't stop using it. I could not even whisper. It was a tough two weeks, but I got creative. I asked for help from others to keep my voice heard. I added an app to my phone that converted text to speech so my co-workers and employees could hear me. I carried pads of paper and markers with me to restaurants and bars to order and "talk" with my friends. I also learned a lot about others as I listened. I realized the power of actively listening to gain a greater understanding of what's being said and how you feel about when you are not allowed to speak.

This experience reminded me of one of my first Fairygodmentors, Michelle Brown Davis. She had a Mona Lisa smile with a wise look in her kind eyes as she led with quiet grace. She would sit in a meeting and take it all in. However, with a sentence or two, she could command the entire room to stop and think about the perspective or idea she brought to the table. It was an art. I wanted to have that command.

One day while on the phone with a manager who wanted me to go above and beyond to hire the right person for their IT team, I was frustrated because it was taking weeks to fill the position. I said very loudly, "Can you believe this guy wants me to part the Red Sea for his team?! Who does he think I am, a miracle worker?!"

Michelle gently pulled me into her office, asked me to take a seat, and then asked if I had a challenging call with a customer. Before I could say, "yes," she said, "I already know because I heard you outside of my office." She smiled very kindly and said, "You've got great ideas and insight, but not everyone in the world needs to hear it. If you need to share anything or need help, come to me directly, and we can discuss." She was teaching me my first lesson in Emotional Intelligence.

I took that feedback and advice to heart, and it served me well through the years. When things get super intense, and you have emotions bubbling up, how you identify them (self-awareness) and how you manage them (self-management) are extremely important not only in maintaining your department's credibility but your own brand. It's best to pause for the cause. Marinate for a moment. Breathe. Be silent. Be still. Check-in with your feelings. Before taking action, ask yourself, "What do I need? or What can I do?" Don't run away from your emotions. It is critical to understand the best time to tackle a conflict with a co-worker or when you need to wait a minute to gather your thoughts.

I learned that the more I ran away from the emotions-the fewer opportunities I had to identify the emotions, deal with the issue causing them, and use my voice effectively. I often missed important information because I was feeling before I was thinking. That's what our minds do- we feel before we think. Being self-aware and managing your reactions are great skills to practice because they will help you be present for others and be kinder and more in tune with yourself.

Active Listening. You can learn a lot from taking a step back and observing the behaviors, responses, and ways others communicate. I became a better friend, Human Resources business partner, people leader, and a better performer because I learned to take a step back and listen- to myself and others.

Oddly enough, I heard people better when I couldn't traditionally use my voice. I also learned better ways to communicate by observing others. I developed a sense of peace by not working so hard to find a response and allowing others to express themselves fully. The threat of losing my voice forever taught me that using my voice wasn't the only way to communicate effectively. I also learned that there is power in silence. Silence is truly golden.

Losing something important makes you appreciate life so much more. Losing my voice was perhaps the best thing that ever happened to me because I could find my voice more deeply. In losing my voice, I was able to find it again. If you've lost your voice, maybe not because of a medical condition, there is hope that you can find your voice through actively listening.

TAKE

FIVE!

1. Imagine losing your voice for two weeks, how would you effectively communicate with others?

_____

_____

_____

_____

_____

_____

_____

2. What are some ways you can grow your comfort level in using your voice more often?

_____

_____

_____

_____

_____

_____

_____

3. When was the last time you actively listened to someone?

_____

_____

_____

_____

_____

_____

4. What did you learn when you stepped back and
   listened?

   _____

   _____

   _____

   _____

   _____

   _____

5. What can you learn about yourself by stepping back naming your emotions, pausing, and listening?

_____

_____

_____

_____

_____

_____

_____

Chapter Three: Just Say NO to LSD - Lead Singer Disease (Delegation)

I had catapulted my career from a Customer Service Representative to a Leadership Development Training Consultant within three years. Others in the organization were designing career progression programs based on how I was paving my career path. Executives were referring employees, at all levels, for me to provide advice to advance their careers. Little did I know, I was developing my career coaching skills even at the beginning of my career!

I was, as my Dad used to say, "On the fast track."

One day, my manager quit unexpectedly, and I was asked to step in to manage the team. I had finally made it to my dream job in Training and Development, and now I was a big-time manager! This opportunity was a chance to be in the spotlight even more. I had fought hard to get into this department and grow. Here I was killing it... I was leading a team of my peers and rocking out the leadership qualities that I was training others to exhibit. I was in my zone!

One day, the heads of the Human Resources and Training departments asked me to create a team builder for over 400 Human Resources professionals. The team builder would increase their business acumen, help them to understand new products, and make it fun and engaging. They assigned other, more tenured managers to report to me and help make this event unforgettable. I had two shots to make magic! One session was in the spring, and the other was scheduled for the fall. These events were my chance to be seen as a major management rockstar!

I love producing creative ideas, and for this project, I created an American Idol meets So You Think You Can

Dance-style event. I knew it was going to be amazing! I had designed an event that incorporated all of the elements that I had been asked to deliver. I asked a lot of questions to find out what my internal customers needed. They needed a break from the day-to-day stressors; they deserved the VIP treatment, the best in edutainment, and to feel like they were honored guests and not at work. I had the whole thing planned. We had free phones, raffle tickets, handouts, and I brought my karaoke machine in case the sound went out. Before we launched the spring event, I ensured everyone knew their roles and completed dress rehearsals. Everything was confirmed for the event, and my team was ready to rock and roll!

Throughout the first session, people asked me if I needed help, and I told them that I was good, but I wasn't good. The leaders I had assigned to manage the crowds were helping themselves to the food and drinks, but they were not helping me. I was running around trying to be everything to everyone. I was trying to make everyone happy, but things were falling apart very quickly.

People who said they knew what was expected of them were magically clueless the night of the event. The raffle tickets were confusing and were not adding fun. Others were standing around watching as things fell apart. There were more winners than phones! How did this all go so wrong so fast?! People on my team kept coming to me for all of the answers... and I didn't know a thing. My mind was blank.

In a moment of clarity, my HR Department Head turned to me and said, "this isn't looking good, Joyel." That was code for "you're crashing and burning, Girl! You need to fix it - Fast!" (As if I didn't know!)

I wanted to run out of the event screaming. My face showed that – my emotions show on my face, so I quickly fixed my face to reflect that I had this under control. I was thinking, "My biggest internal customer is not happy, but I can't freak out now!" I snapped out of it and did the best that I could to salvage the evening. Everyone present ultimately had a great time, but I was aware of the colossal mess going on behind the scenes. It wasn't good.

The next day, after avoiding her all morning, my Training Department Head cornered me and politely said, "That was an interesting evening. What are your plans for the next session?" I told her that I was going to regroup and make it better. But what happened that night?! I intended to host an amazing team builder that educated and entertained the group. The only problem, I was trying to do this on my own. I had LSD. Lead Singer's Disease. After all of my years of singing with various rock groups, I almost forgot that you are nothing without your band.

I couldn't do all of this on my own. I needed to work WITH my team. By pushing them away when they were offering help- I was working against them. I heard them, but I wasn't actively listening to them. When you're under pressure, it is critical that you remember to support others. You have to take a pause for the cause and listen to what's needed without focusing on your thoughts. It is important to summarize what you heard so you can check for understanding. My fifth-grade teacher would say, "Never assume because you make an A$$ out of U and Me." Because of this event, I had to remember some of the lessons I teach other leaders. When things get rough, you need to Show Your Ask and delegate.

Our second event was scheduled for the fall. We don't always get a second chance to fix our first mess. I was determined to make the best of this learning experience. I needed to make sure I took what I learned from the colossal catastrophe and improve it by delegating and communicating what I needed from each event team member.

When showing your ASK during team projects, don't forget to **Show, Tell, and Celebrate**.

SHOW - Define what success looks like to you, the organization, and the team. Paint the picture to help your team see your vision. To gain more team buy-in for projects or deliverables- ask them to help you paint the big picture.

TELL - Complete the following sentences "When this event is over, success will look like..." or "When I'm out of the office, success looks like..." If you can't fill in those blanks, ask your team to fill in the blanks with you. Remind them that the more involved with the planning and execution that they are, the more successful the project will be. Conflict arises from a lack of communication, so communicate often, especially as changes occur. Your team will appreciate your transparency and your ability to keep it real. Create a strategy to communicate about emergencies, issues, or questions, especially on the day of the event.

Make sure you also get input about how they would like to communicate.

CELEBRATE - Celebrate the small wins as you are getting closer to success. Did they push the needle a little further? Did they follow through on the delegated tasks with little direction? Did they proactively produce solutions to problems when they used to come to you with issues? If so, celebrate those small wins and any others that will empower your team to take initiative.

A week after the first session, I met with the support team to discuss what went well and what could have been improved. I did not place blame because I needed to strengthen my team for the fall session... but I also didn't shy away from shedding light on our "opportunities" for improvement. I also encouraged their input by asking questions such as, "How could I have supported you better?"

It was amazing that everyone took accountability for their actions and inactions that night. We all committed to doing better at the next event. They also told me that I needed to step back, stay in my lane, and let them do what they were assigned to do.

I actively listened to all the ideas, and we made decisions as a group. When teams feel included in the plan, it is easier to get buy-in through collaboration — no more LSD. I got the band back together!

I asked a few people to be my ego handlers. They knew I didn't like asking for help and suffered from LSD. It was their job to offer solutions to make things work and get things done. I told them that I trusted their judgment to make things happen, but I also made some contingencies in case things went wrong. I assigned backups to my backups. It is better to be over-prepared than unprepared. We were working in more harmony than ever.

I walked through the new plan of action with the department heads, and they were happy to hear that we had a collaborative strategy to execute the event. Fast forward to the fall. I had surgery a week before the event and promised myself that I wouldn't let that get in the way of me kicking off the second event.

I was cleared to return to work but was ordered to "take it easy." I didn't want others to treat me any differently, but there were times where I needed to sit down and rest. LSD took a back seat, and I had to Show My Ask.

I had to ask for help when I didn't want to give up control. That was hard for me. I learned that giving up control isn't a weakness.-It is a strength, especially when you're asking your teammates to help by leveraging their strengths. Giving others a chance to shine is the key to success.

The second event was a hit and working as a team made it even better! Both department heads were ecstatically happy. My teammates felt empowered by being more involved. The event was duplicated for several other departments because of its success. I remembered to celebrate the success of the event and to thank everyone for their contributions. Don't ever forget to celebrate – even the smallest milestones keep morale high and the band rocking and rolling to success.

TAKE FIVE!

1.　　Have you ever had a case of LSD? Describe what specifically happened?

_____

_____

_____

_____

_____

_____

_____

2.   Can you identify proactively when LSD is slipping into your actions?

_____

_____

_____

_____

_____

_____

3. What gets in the way of you delegating to others or asking for help? How can you repair that block?

_____

_____

_____

_____

_____

_____

_____

4.   What can you stop, start, and continue

regarding delegating to your team members?

_____

_____

_____

_____

_____

_____

_____

5.   Have you practiced self-compassion when you realized you had LSD? (If you haven't done so, make sure you do- you're human. Be kinder to yourself.)

_____

_____

_____

_____

_____

_____

_____

Chapter Four: When You Raise Your Voice, You Raise Your Value
(Giving & Receiving Feedback)

I wouldn't be where I am today without telling people where I wanted to go and who I wanted to be. Speaking up is not about being a bully or a nuisance; but it's about communicating with clear intentions. I'm going to share my million-dollar advice! Every conversation, interaction, and situation will be successful if you *make collaboration and support a priority*.

Ask yourself, "How are we going to work together to create success?" and "Who needs my help today?"

This strategy works for negotiations, creating boundaries, coaching others, giving feedback, and asking for what you want and need in your career and personal life. It is an amazing energy shift. You will be attracting what you want rather than detracting.

Coaching Upward

I remember when I was working on a huge project for the Training Department. It took months to pull it together. My manager had delegated the project to me, and I knew this project could make the team shine. When we were on the national project launch call, my manager discussed the details of the project but took credit for the entire thing! I had a Scooby-Doo reaction-(RHUH?!) The reaction was internal because I didn't want to say anything on the call to embarrass myself or my manager!

Did this guy take credit for all of my work without acknowledging me?! It bothered me, and I was stewing all weekend about it. I decided to practice what I teach in leadership development. I approached the situation from a fact-based perspective. I needed to fix my face and stop rewriting the story I had created in my mind about my manager.

When giving feedback:

1.   **Be Specific:** Describe the situation. When did the incident occur? Where were you? How did it make you feel? What was specifically said?

2.   **Describe the impact:** How did the behavior or action impact you, the organization, and/or the team? When you are sharing this information, focus on the issue or the behavior, not the person.

3.   **Own your feelings:** People may disagree with how you think, but no one can dismiss how you feel. Use "I" statements and discuss how you felt when you witnessed the behavior or action.

4.   **Serve solutions, not problems:** What are you bringing to the table? Are you dishing up more problems, or do you have a plan to move forward? This

is a leadership trait that is a major part of advocating for yourself and your career. Everyone is aware that organizations have problems. However, you will stand out when you present solutions to improve the situation. How are you being proactive to drive a resolution?

5. **Stop! Collaborate and Listen!** Vanilla Ice was right! When we're providing feedback, we need to pause for the cause and remember the collaboration piece of the feedback puzzle. I asked my manager to help me work on ways to move past this situation and continue working together. This helped us to move on and permitted me to let go and trust that we could move forward in the future.

This type of communication works both ways! How well do you receive feedback?! Here are some fix your face tips.

When receiving feedback:

1.   **Remain Open** - You will need to remain open to hear what is being said. Prepare yourself emotionally and remember that *feedback is just information.* They are sharing this information with you because they have either observed, heard, or experienced something that may need to change.

2.   **Actively Listen** - Regardless of the type of information being shared with you, you may have already developed stress and anxiety around this matter. When we stress ourselves out, our ears shut down, and we become defensive. It will be challenging, but you will need to listen actively. While you're listening, take notes to understand and clarify what is being said by repeating what you've heard. "So, what I hear you saying is..."(repeat what was said) to ensure you are on the same page. Other examples include: "So when you said...(repeat what was said), would it be fair to say that you meant... (state what you think) and felt... (state what you think)?" "Have I understood

correctly that when I did...(state what happened), you felt... (state how you think the person perceived it)?"

3.   **Watch your non-verbal cues** - Sometimes, when we are receiving information - especially if it is not positive, we can find ourselves internally shouting back, imagining what to say next, scrunching up our faces, rolling our eyes, sighing... be aware of your non-verbal cues. These non-verbal behaviors show defensiveness and can perpetuate the stereotypes that we are an "angry Black woman," "Nasty woman," or "overly sensitive man." Don't get hooked! And don't smile unless you mean it. Smirking can be equally offensive.

4.   **Focus on the behavior or issue, not the person** - Data is being shared with you. Stay focused on the issue. This conversation is not personal. It may feel personal but focus on the issue and matter at hand. Is there any validity in the information being shared? If you're not clear on the issue or information,

ask for clarity. Confirm your understanding with a summary of the event and the next steps to follow before you leave the discussion. Ask the person giving the feedback to restate what was said if there is disagreement about any points.

5.   **Check Yourself Before You Wreck Yourself** - Emotional intelligence is important when giving and receiving feedback. Check your emotions to remain in tune with your self-awareness. You should be able to execute self-management even when the feedback you receive causes your emotions to rise. ***You have the control... not your emotions.***

To prepare for my meeting, I drafted a script of talking points to share

- how I felt when he shared the project as if he did all the work himself

- how I felt dismissed and not valued

- how I didn't understand why he behaved that way

- its impact on how I felt about doing future projects for someone I had viewed as my mentor for all these years

I wanted to flake out and send these questions to him in an email because I was so nervous about the meeting. Coaching a peer or someone new is one thing but coaching upwards presented a challenge for which I had not yet prepared. Who did I think I was?!

My manager had disrespected me, and I needed to let him know so I could get back to a successful working relationship. This type of conversation was too important to send in an email. I wanted him to understand how his actions impacted me. I needed us to see eye to eye. Otherwise, the tension would remain between us.

I scheduled a meeting to meet with him face to face. No lie, I was really nervous! I rehearsed my talking points with my Aunt Tommye. Family can be a great resource for Fairygodmentors too. She is a great sounding board for role-playing and career advice. We practiced until I could take the emotion of the situation out of the conversation. I stuck to my script, remembered to set the intention of collaboration and support, and shared how I felt. I asked if he could help me move past this so we could work better together. And then- I stopped talking. There was a long... PAUSE. It felt like I was waiting a million years for him to speak.

His face twisted up, and he dropped his head. He was devastated. He apologized profusely and admitted that he did take all the credit for the project. He shared that it wasn't his intention. He assured me that he would make it up to me. I followed up to ensure that he was clear of my intentions. We both identified ways to move forward.

On the next call with the national team, my manager made it a point to say, "I was remiss not to mention something and someone very important to this project. I took credit for work that was done by Joyel Crawford. She worked very hard for several months to pull this project together. I want to thank her for all of her efforts." We were ultimately able to work together better than before. We committed to being more transparent with each other and giving credit where credit is due. What's really interesting is that eventually, I took over his role in leading the team. He saw me as a protégé, and I saw him as a Fairygodmentor. Coaching upward improved our communication which benefited each of us and our team. When you raise your voice-you raise your value.

TAKE

FIVE!

1. How do you view feedback? Is it a positive or negative thing? If you can name it, you can tame it! Get clear on how you view feedback, so you know how to approach it better.

_____

_____

_____

_____

_____

_____

_____

2. How's your giving feedback game? Does it need work, or is it working well? List out what's working and not working for you.

_____

_____

_____

_____

_____

_____

_____

3. How do you receive feedback? Just like gift-giving, how are you receiving the gift of feedback? Tap into those reactions. Does anything need a little extra attention?

_____

_____

_____

_____

_____

_____

_____

4. When you provide feedback, what steps can you take to ensure everyone is on the same page before you end the conversation? Do you have a practice buddy? If not, find one. It doesn't have to be someone at work. Remember my Aunt Tommye? Your buddy may be closer than you think. Practice! It helps with the delivery of feedback.

_____

_____

_____

_____

_____

_____

5. What steps can you take to move forward from the feedback conversation?

_____

_____

_____

_____

_____

_____

Chapter Five: Work Burnout and Self-Leadership

As more tasks and projects piled onto my desk through the years, I was starting to feel overwhelmed. But for fear of looking weak, I didn't say anything. It was like an all-you-can-eat buffet of opportunities to shine and help others, but I was full, and my body was rebelling. I wasn't sleeping well, getting sick a lot, losing my hair, couldn't concentrate and was making some wonky decisions. I was burning out. Me- the big communicator, and I wasn't telling anyone about it.

I remember my first experience with work burnout. It was 18 years into my career. I was five minutes late for my fifth conference call of the day, and my manager called to ask why I was late. I broke down and shared that I was too sick to make it to the call on time. I was all things to all people, and I couldn't do it anymore.

This Rockstar had fallen from grace. I offered to resign from my position that day, but my manager begged me to take a medical leave from work to get the help I needed and stay with the company.

I had to step away from the business to have several stress-related surgeries to resolve what I wasn't sharing with others- I had hustled and flowed until I couldn't hustle or flow no mo!

I wanted to be the best to my team and the projects I committed to, but you can't pour from an empty cup. I had learned the hard way that ***NO is a complete sentence***. I was at full capacity and needed to speak up, say NO, and ask for help. As I've said before, asking for help isn't a weakness. It's the strongest thing you can do to be successful in life.

I learned to practice self-leadership, which isn't always about bonbons and bubble baths but more about how you *think* about leading yourself. It is necessary to use kinder words and remember that if you wouldn't say it to a loved one- you should not say it to yourself. If you're at full capacity, say so. Timing is everything. People need to know when it is a good time to talk or work on something. If you need a break to breathe, say you need a break. **Budget, invest, and protect your time like it is your money!** How are others going to respect your time if you don't respect it?! Speaking up is not only best for your professional development but your personal development as well.

It may not feel like it when you're experiencing it, but you *can* bounce forward from burnout. If you see or feel something- say something. Again, use your effective communication muscle and SHOW YOUR ASK. It's hard to make time to rest and recharge. Use the resources you have available at work or search for free community resources. As the Reverend Dr. Dolly Parton says, "Don't get so busy trying to make a living that you forget to make a life."

How do you create boundaries, ask for help, and say no? It takes time, but it starts with a plan.

1.   **Take a Pause for the Cause** - Sometimes the storm is so noisy you can't hear yourself think. Stop for a moment and think about what's not working. Conversely, think about what is working for you. What do you need at this moment?

2.   **If You Can Name It- You Can Tame It** - Dr. Marc Brackett from Yale University studies and speaks on the topic of Emotional Intelligence. He states if you can name the emotions that you're experiencing, you can regulate and manage them. Focus on the emotions. You could be feeling a lot of emotions at the same time. We tend to layer our emotions, but it's important to peel away the layers of your emotional onion and sit with them for a moment. Don't marinate in your misery; sit with each emotion long enough to identify what's going on.

3.   **Identify Your Needs** - Now that you've named your emotions, what do you need at that moment? Do you need to walk away from the situation? Do you need to breathe? Do you need to eat? I know this sounds basic, but we ignore our basic needs A LOT, especially when emotions are running high.

4.   **Go Back to The Basics** - My husband, Jake, has simple rules for life. He's very chill, and life never seems to rattle him because he's mastered self-leadership. These rules are fundamental and can seem like common sense, but sometimes that is all you need. Get back to the basics. One of the rules is, "If you're hungry - eat." Another is, "If you're tired, sleep." Very simple, but again, when you're in a tsunami of emotions, and you can't think straight – go back to your basic needs.

5.   **Be Gentle with Yourself** ¬ You're not a superhero, even though sometimes you may feel like you're being asked to accomplish superhuman feats

daily. Self-compassion is very important in Showing Your Ask.

TAKE FIVE!

1. When was the last time you stepped back and identified the emotions you were feeling in the moment?

_____

_____

_____

_____

_____

_____

_____

2. Can you remember how you felt when you ignored
    your emotions and kept moving forward anyway?
    What happened? What could you have done
    differently?

_____

_____

_____

_____

_____

_____

3. Why is it challenging to ask for help?

_____

_____

_____

_____

_____

_____

_____

4. What could happen if you asked for help?

_____

_____

_____

_____

_____

_____

_____

5.   What could happen if you didn't ask for help?

_____

_____

_____

_____

_____

_____

_____

Chapter Six: Interviewing Isn't Bragging

Many of my clients struggle with interviewing. I often wonder why being asked questions about their work experience is such a challenge. When I ask them to discuss the root of the issue, I often hear that they feel like they are bragging about their accomplishments. As Muhammad Ali says, 'it's not bragging if it's the truth.' Interviewing is telling a factual story about what you have experienced and accomplished in the past. For the hiring manager, this information helps to predict future behavior and performance.

What gets in the way of us feeling like it's bragging when it's the truth? It is us getting in our own way. If we start by looking at the results-based data that we have in front of us, we will learn that our accomplishments are just that- facts and data.

85

Interviewing is the process of sharing information. That's all it is, and this is the perfect time to brag if you want to call it bragging. An interview is the perfect place to call attention to all the magic you bring to the organization. Don't dull your shine!

How do you get out of your own way and step into your shine? The first step is to track your accomplishments. Do you remember that wonderful DIG Folder that I was talking about in Chapter One? This is where the rubber meets the road. Start documenting your wins incrementally.

At 7 o'clock every night, I document accomplishments, things I'm grateful for, acts of self-compassion, and other memories I want to capture in my celebration journal. This journal can be your evergreen DIG Folder. You can keep your notes and accomplishments either in Apple Notes, Google Keep, voice notes, or use good old-fashioned pen and paper. Whatever you do, document your accomplishments as regularly as possible. Keeping the DIG tracking document open all day helped me to capture accomplishments in real-time. I achieve a variety of wins throughout the day, and this prevents me from forgetting them. Studies have shown that we forget 40% of what we've heard within 24 hours of hearing it. Think about that, what we learn, we forget 40% of it within 24 hours! That's a lot of DIG folder data that's going out of your brain! Make your tools work for you. I want to set you up for success as your use your voice to show a potential employer or department head how amazing you are. Part of interviewing success starts with owning your magic and practicing sharing your stories with a successful mindset.

Own Your Magic!

Look at the beginning of the process. We tend to come down on ourselves before we apply for the darn job! It can be a daunting and overwhelming experience to look at all the different jobs available. I highly suggest job window shopping for only an hour because our Debbie Downer or Dismal Dan voices get in our heads, causing us to lose steam and momentum.

When you look at a job you're interested in, get out of your own way by asking yourself, "*when have I done this*" versus "*can I do this*?" You've got this! You can do this! Advocate for yourself by owning your magic. You may not have worked in that particular industry, but you have the basic skills. What can you highlight and share on your resume, cover letter, and interview that shows how you exhibited these skills? Also, you don't have to check all the requirement boxes before applying. If you're familiar with the software, program, or process- go for it.

They Want You to Win!

Let me spill some interviewing tea- recruiters and hiring managers WANT you to be The One. They want you to be the person that is the best fit for the job.

Some ways they test for The One is through screening calls or behavioral-based interviews such as "Tell me about a time when...." An interviewing professional may put you at ease but don't get too comfortable. Remember to share the whole situation, the actions you took, and how it turned out. Share specific details, including what you said in the situation, even if you know the hiring manager.

I missed a big role because I gave the Hiring Manager the CliffsNotes version of the situation, and I was ultimately passed over for the role. When I could debrief and get feedback on what was missing, she told me I was missing the details. She recounted, "I knew what you did, but I didn't know the specifics of how you did them... that's what I wanted to hear." I was heartbroken, and I could tell she was too. Remember, they want you to be The One. Share specifically how you can make the organization successful by connecting your past experiences and skillsets. **Pro Tip**: Create a Scenario Log by putting your experiences into the STAR (Situation- Task-Action- Result) format. This is interviewing gold, and you will come out looking like Rocky Balboa at the top of the Philadelphia Art Museum steps! Creating Scenario Logs will help you synthesize your results-based accomplishments and will be a great reminder of all that you've done (DIG Folder). You can either review your Scenario Log *before* your interview to prepare or *during* a virtual interview. My Fairygodmentor Celeste Bethel-Purdie shared this amazing nugget many years ago. It has been a game-changer! And you can get super creative with it.

The typical questions asked during an interview fall into the following categories

- Effective Communication
- Team Building
- Working Under Pressure
- Customer Service
- Collaboration

- Problem Solving.

Reading the job descriptions will give you a sneak preview of how to anticipate what they may ask you. Practice answering questions with your Scenario Log several days *before* your actual interviews so you can speak with confidence about your experiences and how your past skills can help the hiring manager predict future performance.

Answer the Questions Not Asked

You may be asked standard interviewing questions but don't walk out of the physical or virtual room without answering the questions not asked, such as:

- why you're a great fit for the organization

- new skills you've acquired in a volunteer capacity

- even though you've never worked in that industry before, how you've managed similar situations in a different industry

- how you're getting certified in a particular program or skill that may not be on your resume

You want to let them know you're The One. ***You're not selling ... you're telling.*** You'll also want to avoid using power-robbing words like "I would," "hopefully," "I try," "I should." Stay out of the 'woulds!' (Sidenote: Keep this in mind when you're speaking up in meetings too!) Answer with confidence, and if you are sharing a mistake you made- share what you learned from it. Remember they want you to be The One- show them!

Let's Briefly Talk about Salary

We won't discuss this topic at great length because many factors contribute to your salary. We can discuss more during a coaching session or workshop to review your specific situation. If hiring managers want to know your desired salary, provide them with a range. And be realistic! Do your research to find out the median salary for the role you're applying for. What is the lowest you will accept not to eat ramen noodles and moon pies for dinner each night? And what is a reasonable high end? The Department of Labor and Payscale.com have research data to help you define your range. If you're applying for an internal position, you may have access to this information but check out Glassdoor, where workers tend to be very vocal about salary. Most HR departments perform a salary comparison to ensure you are aligned with your peers in similar roles. If they ask you what you currently make, don't be quick to answer. In some states, this question is illegal for them to ask. It is best to stick with your range.

You're Interviewing Them Too

Ask questions about what you value- is it autonomy? Is it career development and growth, access to leaders or peers for mentorships? Money? Is it beyond salary- like remote working options, medical benefits, time off, tuition assistance, or childcare?

Show your passion! If the job or opportunity makes your mouth water- show and share it! As a hiring manager, there's nothing more exciting than seeing a candidate share their passion for the role during the interview. Take notice of their response to your passion and ensure you are conveying passion and not desperation. I bombed many interviews because I wasn't expressing my passion to work in that department or company- I was desperate to escape where I was working. That shows too.

Ask them questions. Always have a few questions in your back pocket.

- What is not on the job description that they are looking for in this candidate?

- What is their favorite memory working there?

- What is their leadership style?

- What is their vision for the project, organization, or team?

Find out how passionate they are about working there to get more insight into the culture of that department/organization/team.

Also, monitor your comfort level. Don't fall into the trap of not promoting yourself because you assume the interviewer already knows what you've accomplished because you submitted a resume. Assume they don't. Articulate your experiences in specific instances. Safety Tip: If you don't feel safe or if someone says or does something that makes you feel uncomfortable- Get out of there and SAY SOMETHING! Don't put your safety at risk for a job. It's never worth it.

One more note: It's ok to share your successes and accomplishments but be on the lookout for interviewers who want you to provide them free consulting without hiring you first. You could respond "I would love to share my proposed solutions to your problems once I've started working here." Advocate for your time and talent too!

And never speak poorly of a business partner or former employer! You're bigger than that, and the comments will speak more to your character than the person of whom you are speaking.

Know Your Numbers

Another best practice to advocate for yourself and your career is to know your numbers. It's never a great feeling to be asked about specific results you have achieved, and you don't have the exact data. Once while interviewing for an internal role from Human Resources into Marketing, I thought I had thoroughly researched the department. Right out the gate, the Hiring Manager wanted to know who our competitors were in that division. I assumed it was our overall company's competitors. Nope... each division has different competitors, who have different pricing structures and different target audiences and data points that drive a specific marketing strategy to make more money for the company. Never assume you know everything. Dig a bit deeper to get the data points. Talk to people in the department. Ask them for what looks like success in their world so you can know their numbers too. Learn them, know them and be able to speak to them with confidence. Knowing your professional numbers will also help you in salary negotiation conversations by allowing you to share your results-based achievements and years of experience as supporting evidence for a raise, promotion, or new job.

Present your numbers in a compelling and creative way. When I was interviewing for internal roles, I would create a portfolio of my work and outline my 30-60-90-day plan for the success of the organization and team. This shows the hiring manager or department manager that you know your plan and can explain how you will execute the plan.

How much money did you save or make for the business? How many people were reached? How many subscribers were added? When you know your numbers, you will be better equipped to step into your power and share the value you bring to an organization or team.

Ask for Feedback

Many times, when you don't get the job or promotion, you're left reeling from the sting of rejection. If you want to understand why you weren't selected -ask for feedback. Some companies and hiring managers create the space to provide it. Sadly, some don't and leave you feeling empty and confused. Be easy on yourself! It may not be that you weren't right for the job- perhaps this wasn't the right job for you.

Have you been ghosted? Did you follow up in a week and still haven't gotten an answer? See that ***NO as the Next Opportunity***—their loss. How folks treat you during the interview process is a window into the future. If they treat you poorly as a candidate, think of how they might treat you as an employee! Keep it movin'!

Suppose you receive an opportunity for feedback from an interview? Bravo for landing the feedback call! This type of conversation rarely happens, and it's considered the white whale of professional development. You should view the meeting as an opportunity for collaboration and support. If it's an internal position and you didn't get the job-continue to show up. You can ask the hiring manager questions like: "How can I best support your team?" "What were the specifics skills or experiences that I need to develop to be on your team?" "Are there opportunities or projects that exist where I can still be visible and demonstrate that I'm invested in the role?" Even if you were not selected, sharing that you will continue to show up demonstrates impeccable character. Keep at it! And congratulations for continuing to glow up and grow up.

TAKE

FIVE!

1. On a scale of 1-10, what's your comfort level with interviewing? Why?

_____

_____

_____

_____

_____

_____

_____

2. What do you want to stop, start, or continue to improve your interviewing skills?

_____

_____

_____

_____

_____

_____

_____

3.   List your top results-based achievements.

_____

_____

_____

_____

_____

_____

4. Do you know your numbers? Can you speak to them with confidence? List them here.

_____

_____

_____

_____

_____

_____

_____

5. What would you put in your Scenario Log to
   better prepare to interview with confidence?

_____

_____

_____

_____

_____

_____

_____

Chapter Seven: Mentors, Sponsors, and NASCAR- Oh My!

"How do I get a mentor or sponsor?" This is a question that I am often asked. My simple answer is, "You ask." You are in the driver's seat of your career. You have the power to steer your career in any direction. If you decide you want to change lanes, that's fine. Do it. If you need help getting there, ask for directions. How do you find a mentor or sponsor?

Keep It Simple

Start with the lowest hanging fruit - your manager. Yes, your manager. If you do not have regular check-ins with your manager about your career, you need to start having them as soon as possible. Regular one-on-one meetings with your manager about work and career-related issues will keep you and your career on track. Don't wait for the direction to come from leadership. Be proactive and create your own path.

Think of your manager as the GPS in your career car. You put in the address, and they should help guide you to your planned destination. It is their job. If you want to change direction, you should advise your manager (Your Career GPS) and determine if the route needs to be adjusted. They don't know what they don't know. Once you share your desired change, they can counsel you on the next steps and help you find resources that will aid in your development. Remember that I shared that I knew what I wanted to do and where I wanted to go at the start of my first Big Girl job. It starts with you. ***Showing your Ask*** from the get-go is where you will own control of your destiny.

These regular meetings are also good for coaching upwards. Always have an agenda and take notes. In some instances, your manager may not seem like an ideal fit for coaching you forward or upward. Do not despair. There are strategies to help improve the working relationship.

Do you have a micromanager?

You can open the conversation with, "Do you want me to be productive and successful? Yes, it's a bold question, but it sets the intention of collaboration and support from the beginning. Of course, they are going to say 'yes.' If you don't get a 'yes' – get help from your Human Resources department or your compliance hotline.

You ask this bold question to get them to respond. If they say, "Yes, I want you to be productive and successful," you can reply with "Great! Can we discuss ways to better work together toward making that happen? When I start a new project, I feel like I am being asked hourly to check in on how I'm doing. When I'm stopped for check-ins throughout the day, it interrupts the flow of my productivity. I want to get the project in on time but need uninterrupted time to work on it. What do you think about holding an end of the week check-in meeting so I can keep you posted and stay on schedule?"

Make sure to take notes during all of your one-on-one conversations with your manager. Review what was discussed, and then send a copy of your discussion to your manager. This is useful, especially if you have discussed deadlines, performance, or career pathing— *Document, Document, Document.* Keeping accurate notes of your discussions isn't just for the manager- it also assists you in advocating for your career and holding both of you accountable for your progress.

What if your manager doesn't cut it as a mentor?

If you don't have a great relationship with your direct manager, look elsewhere to identify a better candidate to support your career aspirations. Sometimes it is your manager's manager, someone in a different department, or someone at a different company. Look around you. Who do you admire? What do you admire about them? Are they someone you would like to emulate? What professional brand are they putting out? Is there a project that this person is working on that excites you? Is it someone you have heard speak and you want to connect with? These are people who could be potential mentors or sponsors.

How do you start the mentor conversation?

Most people are like me- flattery operated and have no issues with talking about themselves. It's going to sound a lot like asking someone out on a date but be direct −ask the person if they have time to chat. I suggest scheduling 30 minutes maximum as a time limit for these conversations. First, you want to learn more about this person and their growth within the organization and/or their business. Share that you are interested in learning more about their career path. The rest should flow very easily.

Listen to their responses. How are they talking about others? Are they speaking highly of others when they are not in the room, or are they badmouthing them? Is their outward performance matching what you are seeing and feeling in person? Do you feel like you want to learn more about them, or was this conversation enough to tell you all you needed to know?

If you feel compelled to have more discussions, ask them their availability to have more conversations like this one. If you feel drawn to them and like they can provide substantial advice, ask if they would be open to a mentoring relationship. Remember what my father also used to say, "You don't know unless you ask."

What's the difference between a mentor or a sponsor?

Mentors guide you, and a sponsor will advocate for you. The best analogy is a sport I know nothing about-NASCAR. I know it's popular and it involves cars. But there is something that I *do* know about NASCAR. Each car races around the track with tons of advertisement stickers covering the entire car. Those stickers are sponsors – the folks who have put their brand reputation and money behind that driver. The mentors are the pit crew, the folks offering the driver support, repairs, fuel, and getting the driver back on course to win. The driver is always in control, but they have a support system to help them cross the finish line first.

Finding a Mentor or a Sponsor

I will never forget my most recent professional stalking incident. Wait! Have I told you about professional stalking yet? Well, let me take a step back and explain.

First, no mentors or sponsors were harmed in my courageous pursuit to be mentored by them. Secondly, you must remember you can't go at it alone. Seeking out a mentor is integral to your career and personal growth. Shirley Chisholm spoke about bringing your own folding chair to get a seat at the table. I also believe that you can enlist the help of a master carpenter (mentor/sponsor) to not only help you bring your own folding chair but to help you build your own damn table!

Professional stalking is about taking concerted action to seek out your mentor without breaking the law! I need to say this explicitly because I'm using the word 'stalking.'

I use my Fan Girling energy to fuel my passion for finding the right mentor or sponsor. Yes, I was bold about finding anything or anyone that would help me grow and develop.

My sheer desire to grow and develop in Corporate America blinded me from feeling embarrassed when asking leaders to mentor me. I was simply asking for directions to get me where I wanted to go.

When I was trying to break into the Learning and Development Team, I shared my frustration with my current mentor, who was a Human Resources Executive. She suggested I reach out to the head of the Training Department to discuss my desire to work directly with her in her department. I shared with my mentor that I had difficulty getting her to speak to me. Whenever she would come to the office, I would re-introduce myself and share my passion to be on her team, but that was all I did. My mentor advised me to take more concerted action to get seen by her.

The next time I caught wind that she would be visiting our office, I reached out to the head of the department's assistant to schedule a face-to-face meeting. I brought my resume and my results-based accomplishments aligned with all the training I was proactively developing and facilitating to get the experience to work in her department. After sharing my resume, I asked point-blank, "What else do I need to do to get onto your team?" She shared some suggestions like joining the professional training association, and she said something very important- she asked me to keep in touch with her. She told me that the next time a job opening became available in her department, I should call her, tell her about it, and then post for it - no matter what it was.

I took those directions very seriously. When an opportunity became available, I took her advice - posted for the job, interviewed, and told her when I had applied for the job.

I did not know that she was sponsoring me for an opportunity to be seen by the decision-makers. Although I interviewed for the role and didn't get the position, I had shared my passion, experience that I gained on my own, and my desire to work on the team with the hiring team. I asked them to keep me in mind for future training positions within the department. As discussed, I also shared this information with the head of the department. Within the next month or two, a training role became available, and I applied again. This time, I got the job! Her sponsorship helped me get the role. She put her name and confidence behind my name. She put her sticker on my career car. I grew in that department and ultimately led two territories with their leadership development programming supporting over thirty thousand employees.

Sponsorship isn't something I asked for; however, my ability to deliver results opened the door for it. People saw my passion and determination to get the job done, and they offered me opportunities to shine.

Think back to those NASCAR drivers. The sponsors didn't put their brand on a loser – they put their reputation on the car and driver they believe could win. Your results should show the sponsor that you're the best bet. Know your numbers and show your value!

Professional Stalking

I recall another incident that resulted in me finding a mentor by professional stalking. It was several years before I moved to Philadelphia to be with the man who became my fabulous husband. As I was scoping out the city for opportunities, I saw a sign.

Yes, it was a literal sign on the side of a building advertising a women's leadership development business. I looked up the business online, found the founder, Grace Killelea, and immediately connected with her on LinkedIn. In my invite, I shared that I would be moving to the Philadelphia area shortly, admired what she was doing to advance women in leadership positions, and would be working with her soon. Yes, I told her that I would be working with her.

Share that passion! Her business sounded fabulous, and I felt called to work with her.

Once I moved to Philadelphia, I resigned from my corporate job and began marketing my new business. I only knew one person, my boyfriend. How was I going to launch my coaching and consulting business without knowing anyone? Networking is the way to grow your career and business. I joined a professional organization's chapter that I belonged to when I was working in Corporate America. One of the organizations was having a panel discussion. The keynote speaker was Grace Killelea, the woman who owned the business I predicted I would be working with in the future! As she spoke, she was everything I imagined she would be. She was everything! Her gravitas, her humor, and her command of the room! I HAD to work with her. During the first break, I introduced myself to her. As we walked and talked, I realized I had followed her into the restroom. I didn't follow her into the stall. I do have my boundaries! We still laugh about this first encounter to this day!

After we spoke briefly, she gave me her assistant's number and advised me to set up a formal meeting with her to talk more.

Prior to the meeting, I printed a copy of my resume and a list of questions I wanted to ask her to get to know more about her and the business she created. During the first meeting, a lot of things were revealed. We learned that we had so much in common, from our extensive careers in Human Resources to a passion for leadership development and a talent for public speaking. She was very open to hearing my story and how I ended up in Philadelphia; then, she flat out asked how she could support me. And I *Showed My Ask*.

I shared that I did not know anyone in Philadelphia, and I was at a loss on where to start. I needed a mentor and a sponsor to help me grow my business. She was very gracious and quickly introduced me to several networking groups that generated business leads for me. She and I also set up check-in chats to discuss my progress, and it was refreshing to bounce my business ideas off her. She gave me direction and advice on offerings to provide my clients and helped me develop my niche. She also acted as a sponsor by inviting me to be a member of her faculty to train and develop the amazing women in her leadership development program. My prediction of working with her came true! She was my first official client in Philadelphia. That was many years ago, and she is still cheering me on as an integral part of my professional and personal life. To this day, we send each other business referrals and check in regularly to keep each other encouraged.

Keeping in Touch

It's best to keep in touch with your mentors and sponsors regularly. How much is too much? Ask your mentor or sponsor what a good frequency for them is. I like to stay connected with my support team quarterly. I still reach out to colleagues from previous working environments. I like to say that I am the sock that doesn't get lost in the laundry! When you are developing lasting relationships, like your mentor or sponsor, you want to keep those fires burning. You never know when they may be needed in the future to warm up an opportunity.

One-on-One Meetings

As previously mentioned, there may be times when you change the direction of your career path, and it is up to you to update the address in your Career GPS. How do you do that? Make sure that you tell someone! You can't keep your career a secret. It is important to schedule regular one-on-ones with your manager.

If you're not already- get on their calendar for a standing meeting. Have your agenda prepared with items focused on your career development. It can be a discussion of a project you initiated, a role you are interested in applying for, or changes in where you would like to move. Your career path is not a ladder; it's a lattice. You can move in multiple directions to get where you would like to be.

You can also use these meetings to share best practices that can help optimize team productivity. Pitch it to your manager first to see if you can share the ideas at the next team meeting. This could lead to you shadowing someone or pitching your idea for a promotion or merit increase.

I remember when I transitioned from Customer Service to Human Resources. I was hired to be an Administrative Assistant, but after six months, I realized I was doing a lot more than I was hired to do. The position was less administrative and more analytical. I took a page and, on one side, listed out the job responsibilities I was hired to do. Then drew a line in the middle of the page, and on the other side, I listed all the responsibilities I was asked to do. It was glaringly obvious that I was doing much more than I was hired to produce. I call this the Half-Pager Approach. It was a great business case and visual representation to share with my manager when I asked him about my current roles and what I wanted to continue to explore. He agreed with me and sent it to the Job Evaluation Committee. They approved my job change, and within six months, I went from an Administrative Assistant to an EEO Analyst. It was because I spoke up and Showed My Ask.

TAKE FIVE!

1. How often do you have one on one meetings with your manager? If you are not, what is getting in the way?

_____

_____

_____

_____

_____

_____

_____

2. If you are not having these career development meetings, what can you do to schedule regular meetings with a leader who can help you develop?

_____

_____

_____

_____

_____

_____

_____

3. List some people in your community, company, or life that you admire and would like to have as a mentor.

_____

_____

_____

_____

_____

_____

_____

4. When are you scheduling your mentor or sponsor meeting? Put a day and time on this answer-get it booked!

_____

_____

_____

_____

_____

_____

5. What questions are you going to ask your

potential mentor or sponsor?

_____

_____

_____

_____

_____

_____

One Last Thought

I know I shared a ton of tips and tools to get you started on Showing Your Ask. It can be overwhelming to see so much to do and think about when growing your career. And that's ok. Take your time with each step. Remember that creating change is uncomfortable and takes practice. However, I want you to promise that you will Show Your Ask at least once. Share that moment with me! Take a selfie and tag me, send me an email, or send a carrier pigeon! If you take a small step forward, you're taking courageous action toward creating the career and life you want to live.

Action builds momentum, and that's exactly what you need to drive your vision of success forward.

You got this!

Love, Your Fairygodmentor,
@JoyelCrawford

About the Author:
Joyel Crawford

Armed with two decades' leadership development experience and a passion for inspiring others to action, Joyel Crawford launched Crawford Leadership Strategies in 2014. She believes when we rise into our own power, we can live more authentic experiences – both personally and professionally. With this belief at heart, Crawford Leadership Strategies has provided leadership development training, career coaching, and speaking events for clients, including the United States Senate, The New York Times, ESPN, Intuit, Aramark, the Society for Human Resource Management (SHRM), DC Housing Authority, and numerous schools and universities. As a keynote speaker and leadership consultant, Ms. Crawford's work enhances clients' career paths by providing clarity and confidence in identifying and achieving their goals. Having been described as a "FairyGodMentor," Ms. Crawford has expanded her consulting practice to host the hit podcast "Career View Mirror®." A Certified Professional Career Coach, Ms. Crawford began her professional career shortly after graduating Cum Laude at Elon University with a Psychology degree as an Isabella Cannon Leadership Fellow. Ms. Crawford obtained her MBA from Fairleigh Dickinson University with a concentration in Management. Her career advice is featured in Forbes, The Wall Street Journal, Essence, Newsweek, Huffington Post, The Muse, Girlboss, The Ladders, Yahoo! Finance, Thrive Global, The Chicago Tribune, Capitol Standard, Philadelphia Magazine, XoNecole, Fairygodboss, Next Avenue and many more. You can find Joyel performing on the stage and screen as a professional actor and singer when she's not working. She lives in New Jersey with her amazing husband, Jake.